BLACK VOICES ON RACE
LANGSTON HUGHES

by Chyina Powell

FOCUS
READERS.

NAVIGATOR

WWW.FOCUSREADERS.COM

Focus Readers is distributed by North Star Editions:
sales@northstareditions.com | 888-417-0195

Produced for Focus Readers by Red Line Editorial.

Content Consultant: Christopher Allen Varlack, PhD, Assistant Professor of English, Arcadia University

Photographs ©: Fred Stein/Picture Alliance/DPA/AP Images, cover, 1, 4–5, 26–27; Chyina Powell, 2; Everett Collection Inc/Alamy, 7; AP Images, 8–9, 25; Science History Images/Alamy, 10, 19; Jack Delano/Library of Congress, 12–13, 23; Red Line Editorial, 15; Carl Van Vechten/Library of Congress, 17; Charles J. Olson/The Daily Journal/AP Images, 20–21; Bebeto Matthews/AP Images, 28

Library of Congress Cataloging-in-Publication Data
Library of Congress Cataloging-in-Publication Data is available on the Library of Congress website.

ISBN
978-1-63739-265-2 (hardcover)
978-1-63739-317-8 (paperback)
978-1-63739-417-5 (ebook pdf)
978-1-63739-369-7 (hosted ebook)

Printed in the United States of America
Mankato, MN
082022

ABOUT THE AUTHOR

Chyina Powell is a freelance writer and editor. She is the founder of both Powell Editorial and the Women of Color Writers' Circle and can often be found with a cup of tea and a book in her hand.

TABLE OF CONTENTS

CHAPTER 1

"LET AMERICA BE AMERICA AGAIN"

The American Dream is the belief that all US citizens have an equal opportunity for success. It doesn't matter where people come from or how much money they start out with. Through hard work, anyone can be successful.

Langston Hughes disagreed. He published "Let America Be America

Langston Hughes used poetry to share his ideas about the American Dream, freedom, and more.

Again" in 1936. In this poem, Hughes speaks for poor white people. He speaks for Black Americans and Indigenous peoples. He speaks for immigrants. Hughes says the American Dream was never available to them. Slavery, greed, and unfair treatment kept it from them. But Hughes ends the poem with hope. He hopes that one day the American Dream will be a reality. It will be something the **disadvantaged** can achieve.

Langston Hughes was a Black American poet. His poems were about the Black experience. Over the years, he published poetry, plays, and essays. He spoke to audiences about race.

Hughes (bottom right) joins other Black poets at a
Jackson State College festival in Mississippi in 1945.

Hughes won many awards for his
poetry and other writings. His poetry is
read around the world. His work has been
translated into many languages. Hughes
helped shape American literature.

CHAPTER 2

EARLY LIFE

James Mercer Langston Hughes was born on February 1, 1901, in Joplin, Missouri. He went by the name Langston. He was raised mainly by his grandmother. When she died, Langston went to live with his mother. He was a teenager at the time. He and his mother moved a lot. They finally settled in Cleveland, Ohio.

Langston Hughes lived in Lawrence, Kansas, with his grandmother after his parents separated.

Langston wrote his first jazz poem while he was in high school. It was called "When Sue Wears Red."

In high school, Langston submitted his writing to magazines. Usually, he was rejected. But he didn't give up.

Hughes graduated from high school in 1920. Soon after, his first poem was published. It is titled "The Negro Speaks of Rivers." The poem honors the rich **cultures** of Africa. It recognizes the contributions that those cultures have made throughout history.

HUGHES'S BIG BREAKS

In 1925, Hughes lived in Washington, DC. He worked as a busboy at a hotel restaurant. While working, he met popular poet Vachel Lindsay. Hughes shared his poetry. Lindsay enjoyed Hughes's work. He decided to promote Hughes's poetry. Thanks to Lindsay, Hughes received more attention. Later, Hughes gained Charlotte Mason as a patron. This meant she supported him financially. Mason's support allowed Hughes to focus on his writing. However, she tried to influence his writing. Hughes eventually stopped working with her.

CHAPTER 3

WRITING BLACK LIFE

Langston Hughes saw poetry as a way to express himself. He wrote about what he felt. He also wrote about what he experienced. For example, Hughes experienced **racism** firsthand. He had moved around a lot as a child. So, he'd seen how Black people were treated in different places.

Langston Hughes traveled to other countries in addition to other states. He spent time in Mexico, Haiti, Japan, and elsewhere.

Hughes also saw that most works were not written for Black people. Instead, most books, plays, and poems were written with white audiences in mind. Many works did not include Black people at all. If they did, they often presented Black people negatively. They used **stereotypes**.

Hughes could not separate his personal experience from the Black experience. For that reason, he used his poetry to **condemn** racism. For example, he wrote "Open Letter to the South." In the poem, Hughes asks for equality. He asks readers to focus on unity. He states that unity is strength.

Hughes also wanted to let Black Americans know they mattered. He wanted to show the joys and trials of everyday Black life. And he wanted all Black people to be comfortable with who they were. He wrote, "We younger Negro artists who create now intend to express our individual dark-skinned

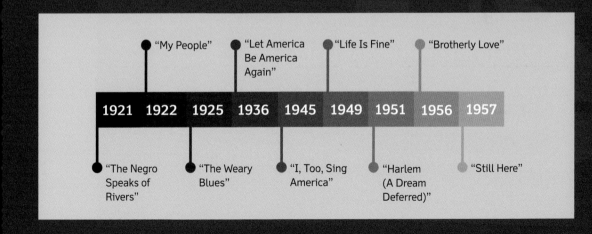

SELECTED POEMS

"My People" — 1922

"Let America Be America Again" — 1936

"Life Is Fine" — 1949

"Brotherly Love" — 1956

1921 1922 1925 1936 1945 1949 1951 1956 1957

"The Negro Speaks of Rivers" — 1921

"The Weary Blues" — 1925

"I, Too, Sing America" — 1945

"Harlem (A Dream Deferred)" — 1951

"Still Here" — 1957

selves without fear or shame. If white people are pleased, we are glad. If they are not, it doesn't matter. We know we are beautiful."[1] These values inspired Hughes's work.

JAZZ POETRY

Hughes loved jazz and blues music. He saw these **genres** as uniquely African American. He felt they showed Black creativity in turning hardship into art. These genres influenced Hughes's poetry. For example, he wrote about jazz. He used **rhythm** and language to create poems that sounded like jazz. This form of poetry is known as jazz poetry. It first became popular during the 1920s. It is still written and performed today. Poets often read their poetry while jazz music plays.

1. Hughes, Langston. "The Negro Artist and the Racial Mountain." *Poetry Foundation*. Accessed March 4, 2022. www.poetryfoundation.org.

Hughes worked with important Black writers on *Fire!!*
They included writer Zora Neale Hurston (pictured).

In 1926, Hughes helped create a magazine for this purpose. The magazine was called *Fire!!* It recognized the importance of Black people sharing their own experiences. The magazine was written by, for, and about Black people. Wallace Thurman edited the magazine.

THE HARLEM RENAISSANCE

Langston Hughes was an important writer of the Harlem Renaissance. This cultural movement lasted from the 1910s to the 1930s. During this time, many Black Americans moved from the South to the North. They also moved from rural areas into cities. This shift was called the Great Migration. It brought many changes.

One was a cultural change. Black artists, writers, and musicians created works about and for Black people. These works challenged white society's stereotypes of Black people. The stereotypes suggested Black people were lazy and violent. But Black creatives took control of their own stories. Their works showed all forms of Black life. Black Americans also formed their own

Langston Hughes (left) stands with other writers and civil rights activists of the Harlem Renaissance.

newspapers, journals, and neighborhoods. They claimed a voice in media.

The Harlem Renaissance encouraged Black people to be proud of their race. Black people grew more confident. Some of them formed civil rights organizations. These organizations included the National Association for the Advancement of Colored People (NAACP). They worked for equality and fair treatment. They helped bring about the civil rights movement in the 1950s.

A PICTORIAL
HISTORY
of the
Negro in
America

Langston Hughes & Milton Meltzer

1000 ILLUSTRATIONS FROM PRINTS, ENGRAVINGS, PHOTOGRA

, with rifle) at the battle of Bunker Hill.

, South Carolina, 1778.

59

CHAPTER 4

BLACK PRIDE

Langston Hughes is known for his poetry. He also broke barriers. Hughes was the first Black American to earn a living by writing and giving educational talks. He made enough money doing both that he needed no other job. He showed Black people they could earn a living through their art.

Langston Hughes's poetry, plays, and essays changed American literature.

Hughes wrote to celebrate Blackness his entire life. He also wrote books about his life. *The Big Sea* was published in 1940. In this book, Hughes said he saw himself as both Black and American.

HUGHES AND THEATER

In addition to poetry, Hughes wrote several plays. *Tambourines to Glory* is one example. It appeared on Broadway in the 1960s. Other people wrote plays inspired by Hughes's poetry. For example, Lorraine Hansberry wrote *A Raisin in the Sun*. The play's title comes from the poem "Harlem." In the poem, Hughes asks what happens to dreams that are not allowed to be achieved. He wonders if they dry up like raisins in the sun. Hansberry's play explores working-class Black life in 1940s Chicago.

Actors rehearse one of Hughes's plays in Chicago, Illinois, in the 1940s.

He wrote, "I was only an American Negro—who had loved the surface of Africa and the rhythms of Africa—but I was not Africa. I was Chicago and Kansas City and Broadway and Harlem."[2] Many Black audiences loved his work. They recognized that he wrote to them and for them.

2. Hughes, Langston. *The Big Sea*. Accessed on Project Gutenberg Canada, March 3, 2022. gutenberg.ca.

But American society was changing. The civil rights movement gained national attention in the 1950s. Black people protested for equal rights. They worked to end segregation. This was the legal separation of people in daily life. Under segregation, white people and Black people went to different schools. They ate at different restaurants. The civil rights movement ended this separation.

Around the same time, the Black Power movement began. This movement was about racial pride and **empowerment**. Supporters wanted Black people to be self-reliant. They didn't think joining white society was enough to end racism.

Some US lawmakers worried Hughes was too radical. They thought his ideas on class were un-American.

Instead, they felt white society needed to change. In this context, some Black people began feeling differently about Hughes's work. They criticized Hughes for not being more **radical**. But Hughes believed in people coming together. He wrote, "*Most* people are generally good, in every race and in every country where I have been."[3]

3. Hughes, Langston. *The Big Sea*. Accessed on Project Gutenberg Canada, March 3, 2022. gutenberg.ca.

CHAPTER 5

WRITING HIS WAY INTO HISTORY

Langston Hughes died on May 22, 1967. At his funeral, jazz and blues music played. Hughes had not been a musician. But he loved music. It had inspired many of his poems.

During his lifetime, Hughes worked with talented artists. For example, he worked with the famous Black musician

Langston Hughes holds one of his records in 1954.

Hughes's home in New York City's Harlem neighborhood was declared a historic landmark in 1981.

Duke Ellington. Ellington wrote a musical piece to go with Hughes's poem "Heart of Harlem."

Hughes also earned many awards. For example, the NAACP gave him the Spingarn Medal in 1960. This award goes to the African American who had the greatest achievements of the previous year.

Hughes published until he died, and his legacy lives on. Hughes is known for being a voice of the Harlem Renaissance. He was an innovator in jazz poetry. He is remembered as a great American poet.

HUGHES AND SIMPLE

In the 1940s, Langston Hughes began writing for the *Chicago Defender*. This is an African American newspaper founded in 1905. Hughes wrote scenes about a Black man named Jesse B. Semple. The character came to be known as Simple. In the scenes, Simple talked to another man. The conversations were often funny and engaging. But they got readers to think about racism. Through Simple, Hughes explored ideas of race and class.

FOCUS ON
LANGSTON HUGHES

Write your answers on a separate piece of paper.

1. Write a paragraph describing what you learned about the Harlem Renaissance.

2. Do you think poetry can change society? How?

3. What is the name of Langston Hughes's first published poem?

   A. "Let America Be America Again"
   B. *Fire!!*
   C. "The Negro Speaks of Rivers"

4. How might the Great Migration have contributed to the Harlem Renaissance?

   A. Black people gathered in northern cities, where they could form a cultural movement.
   B. Black people moved to the South, where they wrote about the white experience.
   C. Black people spread out across the country and lost a sense of Black culture.

Answer key on page 32.

GLOSSARY

condemn
To express disapproval of something.

cultures
Groups of people and the ways they live, including their customs, beliefs, and laws.

disadvantaged
Having fewer resources or opportunities than others.

empowerment
Giving someone the power or ability to do something.

genres
Categories of music, such as jazz, hip-hop, and soul.

racism
Hatred or mistreatment of people because of their skin color or ethnicity.

radical
Having extreme ideas about a topic.

rhythm
In poetry, the mix of short and long phrases to create a certain flow of words.

stereotypes
Overly simple and harmful ideas of how all members of a certain group are.

TO LEARN MORE

BOOKS

Harris, Duchess, and Martha London. *The Harlem Renaissance*. Minneapolis: Abdo Publishing, 2020.

Latham, Irene, and Charles Waters. *Dictionary for a Better World: Poems, Quotes, and Anecdotes from A to Z*. Minneapolis: Lerner Publishing, 2020.

Smith, Sherri L. *What Was the Harlem Renaissance?* New York: Penguin Workshop, 2021.

NOTE TO EDUCATORS

Visit **www.focusreaders.com** to find lesson plans, activities, links, and other resources related to this title.

INDEX

Answer Key: 1. Answers will vary; **2.** Answers will vary; **3.** C; **4.** A